DC PHOTO BOOK

An Insider's View of Washington, DC

Stephen R. Brown

DC PHOTO BOOK: An Insider's View of Washington, DC

THIRD EDITION: Expanded to 160 pages
ISBN 978-0-9766150-9-5
© Stephen R. Brown 2016
202.667.1965
Email: srb@srbphoto.com
www.srbphoto.com

Photographs Copyright Stephen R. Brown
Text by Caitlin Brown • Design by Jane T. Howitt

Table of Contents

Introduction

Washington, DC is a photographer's paradise. Its low-lying landscape is dictated by the highest building in town—the Washington Monument. The publicly funded architecture is wonderfully ornate, and thanks to the abundance of sky and light, the ever-changing shadow and color make for endlessly interesting views. I always have a camera when I cruise the city, and many of these photographs were taken on spontaneous drives around town.

Many of the Insider's Views images were taken on assignment for some of the world's major magazines and newspapers, including *Smithsonian, Life, Time, Newsweek, U.S. News and World Report,* and *The Washington Post*. All have headquarters or offices right here in the District. As a contributor to these publications and a member of the White House News Photographers Association and the United States Senate Gallery, I have had the opportunity to wander and explore where most citizens cannot. I am also a "friend" of the Guild of Professional Tour Guides of

Washington, DC. To DC enthusiasts, this book is but a cursory glance. This city is a stimulating environment and an amazing place to live, work and photograph. My book "WWII Memorial: Jewel of the Mall" has sold over 200,000 copies and made me the happy acquaintance of thousands of Honor Flight™ Volunteers.

My daughter Caitlin (writing), my wife June (editing), Jane Howitt (design) and Jessica Warren worked with me to put the book together. Ellen Gold, past President of the Guild of Professional Tour Guides, gave the book several readings for historical and factual accuracy. Mary Pettinato of Honor Flight Chicago and Jeffrey Wilkes of "This Old School" were also kind enough to read over the manuscript. Jeff Miller, co-founder, and Dave Nichols, board member of Honor Flight™ were readers and supporters throughout the printing process. If there are remaining errors, I take full responsibility. As credited, Jeff Tinsley of Smithsonian provided the Mall aerials and Carol Highsmith, the aerial of the Korea Memorial through her Library of Congress collection.

Part I:
National Mall

United States Supreme Court

On a chilly day in December 1998, Native American rights activists gathered at the steps of the Supreme Court, taking a stance to express their opinions on the case that would be argued that morning, Minnesota v. Mille Lacs Band of Chippewa Indians. For DC natives, a demonstration like this is a relatively common occurrence. From the Jay Court to the present, Americans have brought their political views to the foot of the building to express their views on everything from foreign policy to civil rights. The Supreme Court building was erected in 1935 and has since been designated a National Historic Landmark.

Historians often discuss the Supreme Court according to who was Chief Justice at the time, as the nature of the court's decisions depends hugely on the views of its nine members.

United States Capitol

Sitting on the West lawn of the Capitol during summer concerts and events, visitors to the Capitol stare, enchanted, at the stunning example of American Neoclassic architecture that towers above them. The Capitol's impressive exterior size and soaring dome reflect its importance as both a functional building and symbolic structure. Inside this facade lies a forum in which the world's most influential leaders have debated and formed the decisions that have shaped the history and development of our country. The Senate occupies the Capitol's north wing, and the House of Representatives occupies the south. The Eastern Front overlooks a newly renovated entrance that serves as the traditional entrance for visiting dignitaries. The building's interior abounds with art depicting historic figures and symbols of the United States.

Beyond clear political importance, the Capitol also occupies a unique geographic position in the city, as the building's location atop Capitol Hill intersects the district's four quadrants.

Insider's View

INAUGURATION. On January 20, 1981, Ronald Reagan broke tradition and changed history, taking the oath of office on the terrace of the Capitol's West Front (top left). The day celebrated the Republican victory in both the White House and the Senate, as well as the Iranian rebels' release of American hostages. In his inaugural address, Reagan famously reminded the American people, "To a few of us here today, this is a solemn and most momentous occasion; and yet, in the history of our Nation, it is a commonplace occurrence. The orderly transfer of authority as called for in the Constitution routinely takes place as it has for almost two centuries and few of us stop to think how unique we really are."

How better, then, to capture the distinctiveness of the Americans who gathered on the National Mall on that surprisingly mild January morning than through an equally unique photograph? The National Park Service helicopter is the only aircraft allowed to fly over the Mall on Inauguration Day, so aerial images of the Presidential Inauguration and ceremonies are coveted by photographers. Through this aerial view, taken exclusively from a National Park Service helicopter for Life Magazine, Brown captured the full effect of the sea of Americans gathered for a celebration of such historical import.

"Standing here," remarked Reagan in closing, "one faces a magnificent vista, opening up on this city's special beauty and history. At the end of this open mall are those shrines to the giants on whose shoulders we stand."

Later in Reagan's presidency, another momentous event took place on the Mall (bottom left). This time, however, people gathered at the base of the Capitol in a rally for women's rights and gender equality.

American Veterans Disabled for Life Memorial

The memorial is located within a stone's throw of the Capitol and a fitting salute to disabled Veterans of all wars. It also serves as a reminder to the country's leaders of the high costs our Veterans bear in times of conflict. This memorial is "designed to pay tribute to all disabled Veterans, past, present and future who have served or will serve in our nation's military forces." Walls of laminated glass with text and images surround a star-shaped pool whose central design elements are a ceremonial flame and a pool of remembrance.

National Gallery of Art

The National Gallery of Art is comprised of two buildings with distinctive exteriors that reflect the diverse collections housed within. The newer East Wing, whose modern exterior appears in these photographs, was designed by I.M. Pei and completed in 1978 to house a collection of modern and contemporary art. The East Wing serves as an addition to the original West Wing, founded in 1937 by Andrew Mellon to showcase American and European Art of different media from the 12th to 20th centuries.

Created by a joint resolution of Congress the gallery opened to the public in 1941 after Mellon's death. The collection contains over 109,000 pieces.

National Museum of the American Indian

Since its opening in 2004, the Smithsonian National Museum of the American Indian has become an unmistakable symbol on the National Mall. The building's yellow Kasota limestone exterior and curvilinear shape stand in contrast to the traditional architectural structures in its vicinity. Inside, the lack of sharp corners emphasizes the center's organic fluidity, which reflects the Native American concept of unity with the environment. Many of the museum's employees are of Native American descent.

Pennsylvania Avenue

The traditional path for parades and protests, the route of the inaugural march for every president since Thomas Jefferson, Pennsylvania Avenue connects the United States Capitol and the White House. Pennsylvania Avenue is home to the Newseum (bottom, far right) and runs adjacent to the West Wing of the National Gallery of Art (bottom, near right), both of which have clear views of the nearby Capitol building. The Navy Memorial (top, near right) and the Newseum™ are also avenue landmarks.

Famous marches down Pennsylvania Avenue include a parade for women's suffrage led by activist Alice Paul and a march for unemployment aid during the 1890s depression led by Jacob Coxey. The avenue is also famous for Presidential Inaugural parades (and sometimes walks) by Presidents as they leave the Capitol Inauguration and proceed to the White House.

National Archives

"This building holds in trust the records of our national life and symbolizes our faith in the permanence of our national institutions." These words, engraved on the east side of the National Archives Building, perfectly capture the symbolic and practical function of the site that stores the records of our country's past. Inside the elegant columns and bronze doors of the building lie the three most important documents in the establishment of the United States: the Declaration of Independence, the Constitution and the Bill of Rights. Also housed in the archives is the Magna Carta, which dates to 1297. Together, these four documents are displayed in the Rotunda for the Charters of Freedom, the main chamber open to visitors.

The National Archives' permanent exhibition is known as the Public Vaults. It contains at any given time about 1100 records in documents, drawings, films, maps and sound recordings. Temporary exhibits feature artifacts from outside collections, which visitors view along with lectures or film series.

Insider's View

PRESERVATION. Active preservation is one of the most important tasks performed within the walls of the National Archives Building, as protection and conservation of important documents such as the Declaration of Independence involves more than simple storage.

Visitors to the Rotunda view the documents through hardened glass. As indicated in this rare photograph taken before the Archives were renovated, the documents were raised for viewing during the day and then lowered back into an allegedly "nuclear proof" vault at night for safekeeping. In an emergency, the documents could be lowered from their viewing position in the Atrium above into a steel vault, at which point gi-

ant steel doors would close over the documents. With the increased security of the renovation, the Archives will not reveal their new methods of securing the documents after viewing hours.

The Declaration of Independence, the Constitution and the Bill of Rights have occupied the space in the Rotunda since 1952. Officials placed the documents into airtight encasements filled with inert argon gases, a protective measure designed to preserve the documents for as long as possible. Conservators perform routine checks of the documents and the cases that hold them. Recent electronic advances have augmented these inspections.

Sculpture Garden

The playful blue bristles of Claes Oldenburg's typewriter eraser are visible from every corner of the National Gallery of Art Sculpture Garden, reminding visitors that not every statue in this capital city follows the classic mold. Oldenburg's modern piece stands among the works of Miró, Calder and others in a series of modern and contemporary pieces that provide a refreshing break from the traditional edifices that dominate the National Mall.

Completed in 1999, the Sculpture Garden boasts 17 major works of contemporary art. A large fountain adorns its center, the site for the Jazz in the Garden summer concert series. In the winter, the fountain is converted into a skating rink, making the garden a popular spot for visitors year round.

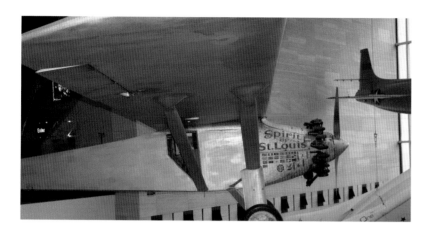

National Air and Space Museum

The most popular of the Smithsonian museums, the National Air and Space Museum houses the world's largest collection of historic air and spacecraft. Notable displays include the Apollo 11 command module, the Spirit of St. Louis, the Wright Flyer and a moon rock from the Apollo 17 mission.

Originally called the National Air Museum, the building was renamed after the huge advances in space exploration achieved during the Space Race of the 1960s. In fact, visitors learn specifically about the competition between the United States and the Soviet Union in an exhibition called Space Race.

Visitors to the museum also have access to twenty-one other exhibition galleries, an IMAX theater, flight simulators and a café. Additionally, the museum's Udvar-Hazy Center (page 156) near Dulles Airport houses and displays an additional part of the collection, which shortly after opening exceeded the space limitations of the National Mall facility. Most museums similarly maintain facilities outside the city to store their excess treasure.

Hirshhorn Museum

Before they enter the museum, the four-acre, two-level Sculpture Garden outside the Hirshhorn Museum provides visitors with a prelude to the 11,500 pieces within. The garden teems with modern and contemporary sculptures, from Rodin's famous bronze figures to di Suvero's minimalist industrial creations. The museum's ultra-modern exterior is no coincidence — architect Gordon Bunshaft intended for his design to stand out among the traditional structures on the National Mall, as he knew the artwork within its walls would be anything but conventional.

Opened in 1974, the Hirshhorn is the first museum in the District devoted solely to modern art, focusing with particular emphasis on contemporary art from the last quarter of the 21st century through the present. Though critics consider its collection of 19th and 20th century sculpture to be its strongest aspect, the museum also lays claim to many modern masterworks of painting, including works by Richter, Bacon and Man Ray.

Smithsonian Castle

The first building on the National Mall, the Smithsonian Castle was designed by architect James Renwick, Jr. in 1847 as the anticipated focal point of the Mall. The Arts and Industries Building borders it on the East, and to its West stand the Freer Gallery of Art and the National Museum of African Art.

An extensive series of gardens and walkways surrounds and links these museums, and all are located along Independence Avenue, a major street that runs east to west and attracts heavy traffic throughout the week. The avenue is a major leg of the Presidential motorcade's usual route to the Capitol.

The Smithsonian Institution was originally constructed according to the will of James Smithson, a British scientist who never actually visited the United States. This particular bequest is perhaps a testament to his Enlightenment-era vision of democracy and education, which he felt would be best fulfilled in America.

United States Holocaust Memorial Museum

Dedicated in 1993, the museum has served as a memorial to the Holocaust and a reminder of the horrors of genocide. Through a combination of federal funding and private donations, the Holocaust Museum contains a number of permanent and traveling exhibitions, and it provides educational outreach and commemorative events throughout the year. Since its opening, the museum has drawn upwards of 30 million visitors from all over the world, a figure that – according to the museum website – includes 91 heads of state. From photographs of Auschwitz to a number of artifacts to video content, the museum collections and archives present the viewer with an experience that is both emotionally charged and educational.

Sculpture on the right: *Loss and Regeneration*, 1993. The United States Holocaust Memorial Museum, Washington DC. Gift of Ruth and Albert Abramson and Family; In Memory of the Children Who Perished in the Holocaust © 1993 Joel Shapiro/Artists Rights Society (ARS), New York.

Bureau of Engraving and Printing

Not to be confused with the United States Mint, the building responsible for the production of coins, the Bureau of Engraving and Printing has been producing paper currency since the 1860s. Each year, billions of dollars are printed at this branch of the U.S. Department of the Treasury and delivered to the Federal Reserve System for circulation. On a tour of the facility, visitors learn how a blank sheet of paper is transformed into an authentic U.S. Treasury bill. The bureau also produces important secured documents for other branches of the federal government.

African American Museum

A stunning new addition to the North side of the National mall is the Smithonian 's National Museum of African American History and Culture. In the background is the Old Post Office Tower which overlooks the city and Pennsylvania Ave. The museum has an observation deck which should make for some of the most exquistie views of the National Mall. Situated so as to catch the firery glow of the setting sun, it is fast becoming an insider's view of the city. It is said to be the last building to be put up on the National Mall but that claim has been made before. Building on the Mall always seems to be controversial and there is a battle afoot about funding and finishing the Dwight D. Eishenhower Memorial.

The White House

Even with enhanced security measures, 1600 Pennsylvania Avenue still receives thousands of visitors a day. Visitors to the White House, the home of the first family and workplace of the President, have the chance to view several of the 132 rooms of different designs and themes.

John Adams was the first president to live in the White House, moving in shortly after its construction was completed in 1800. Architect James Hoban's design was chosen in a contest out of nine submissions, including an anonymous one by Thomas Jefferson. Today, the mansion consists of the Executive Residence, the East Wing and the West Wing, where the President's Oval Office is located. The White House also boasts many recreational facilities and the South lawn is a secure facility for parties.

Pennsylvania Ave View of the White House.

President Reagan and wife Nancy head for Camp David, the Presidential Retreat in 1984.

Early AM at the Northern side of the White House where most political protests occur.

Washington Monument

Staring up at this marble obelisk, visitors will notice a slight color change that begins about 150 feet from the monument's base and wonder if this was part of architect Robert Mills' master plan. Construction of the monument to honor Washington began in 1848. The gradient line marks where construction stopped in 1854 due to a lack of funding. When construction resumed in 1879, the original stone was unavailable, so builders used a slightly different marble visible in the darker color of the top two- thirds of the monument.

Apart from its color, the Washington Monument carries other hues of intrigue – one of which is its height. Extending 555 feet into the DC skyline, the structure towers over much of the District's low-lying landscape. Many residents believe that no building in the city can legally be taller than the Washington Monument, but the "law" is actually just a rumor. This popular misconception only serves to underscore the significance of the monument, a tribute to our founding father and the values upon which this country stands.

Not only is the Washington Monument a powerful icon, it is an ever-present symbol on the DC skyline. As one enters the District, be it by car or by train, by land or air or sea, the obelisk is often his very first glimpse of the city so rich in history. Children know it from an early age as "The Giant Pencil" and learn that the monument remembers a leader who embodied the defining values of our nation today. Even its reflection in the Reflecting Pool, which extends to the Lincoln Memorial, is an icon of elegance and grace.

The monument was completed in 1884 and opened to the public in 1888 after finalization of the interior. After the years of debate and struggle for continued funding in Congress, the structure's total cost came to just over a million dollars. At one time visitors could climb the breathtaking 897 stairs to reach the top. Today, however, the elevator is the only option for visitors without a special permit. Either way, the view is well worth the ascent.

Insider's View

LOST HISTORY. As the security measures on the National Mall increase, access to the best vantage points, such as the rooftops of monuments and memorials, becomes a near impossibility. Taken in 1981, this photograph captures the Independence Day fireworks with the Capitol and the Washington Monument aligned in the background, the Washington Monument elegantly mirrored in the Reflecting Pool. Before security was heightened, the Park Rangers usually gave credentialed photographers access to the roof of the Lincoln and Jefferson Memorials so they could document the fireworks in unique and historical views.

For many photographers, a successful fireworks photograph depends on one or more distinctive reference points, such as a monument or an official building. On the National Mall, however, this is becoming an increasingly difficult objective. Many photographers wonder whether shots like this and the pages that follow will become impossible if security trends continue. The White House News Photographers Association was formed so that photographers could present a united front to White House officials, bureaucrats and members of the five police forces in DC who are restricting access to these treasured views.

To get the photograph on pages 48-49, I waited for a repair to finish on the WWII Memorial wall and arranged a ride on a cherry picker. I love this particular photograph because it is a unique view of the Mall and a historical moment in time. I am always amazed that Washington, DC does not have a full-time photographic team documenting the city's history.

To say that the construction of Memorials is "contentious" is to understate the case. While they are being planned and constructed, editorials pro and con are common and the city's coffee houses are abrew with discussion of the newcomers to the city's skyline. I have noticed that we come to love all our monuments!

WWII MEMORIAL: Jewel of the Mall

The WWII Memorial was signed into law in 1994. but construction was delayed for eight contentious years (page 53). Architect Friedrich St. Florian's winning design was challenged over and over and finally the columns were reduced from the orignal 35 foot height to a more manageable 16 feet. The columns representing the states are organized by order of the states' entry into the union so that Delaware is the first column on the Southwestern left side and Pennsylvania the next on the Northwestern side. They then alternate back and forth by order of entry into the Union.

There are two sets of four eagles in the Atlantic and Pacific Pavilions Each group of four lifting a victory wreath forming what is known as a "Baldachino" or sculptural cover. All of the fixtures --drainpipes, wreaths and eagles-- were made in three foundries in a short two years time using the "lost wax" process (page 58). The twenty-four bas reliefs display scenes from the battles, wartime activites and the Homefront which was in full support of the war. As the Memorial was close to finishing, many Veterans sat in lawn chairs just outside the construction site watching the progress It was amazing to document the construction of this Memorial and even more amazing watching WWII Veterans visit their Memorial.

Photo by Jeff Tinsley, Smithsonian.

Insider's View

CONTROVERSY. In 1994, President Clinton signed a resolution stating that the World War II Memorial must be located on the National Mall, despite limited space and the danger of interrupting an area of utmost historic import. Officials considered three sites, ultimately selecting the Rainbow Pool. The decision, made public on October 5, 1995, sparked immediate controversy.

Located directly between the Lincoln Memorial and the Washington Monument, the Rainbow Pool site historically allowed for an unbroken view between the two landmarks, and construction of a memorial on these grounds would obstruct the line of sight. Furthermore, the space near the reflecting pool and Constitution Gardens is a historic site for demonstrations and marches. If a World War II Memorial had existed in 1963, how would 250,000 people have been able to march on the Rainbow Pool site to hear Martin Luther King's "I Have a Dream" speech? Despite such misgivings, the construction process not only continued – it was actually expedited in order to allow as many World War II veterans as possible to view the memorial, given that the majority were around the age of 80. Congress passed legislation that exempted the memorial from further review and dismissed legal challenges to the design, curtailing the normally lengthy approval process.

In response, critics formed the National Coalition to Save Our Mall. In the introduction to a January 2000 web article entitled "The World War II Memorial Defaces a National Treasure," the coalition of critics and veterans asserted that the memorial "drives a wedge between the Washington Monument and the Lincoln Memorial, breaking the connection between the nation's two most prominent symbols of democracy."

Today, the Memorial columns are sixteen feet high, twenty feet lower than the original design and the structure has become the most-visited memorial in the city. Proponents of the existing design suggest that rather than blocking the view between the Lincoln and the Washington, the columns frame the skyline vista.

Making a Memorial

There is something grand about the sculptural process and so I chose a grand structure to document the "lost wax process". Two years of photography ultimately became a unique book. It celebrates the finished Memorial and the craftsmanship that went into this Memorial. On the far right you can see the 18 and 1/2 foot high bronze eagles being assembled and below, the finished bas reliefs which illustrate the war in bronze carvings. Lower right, the first step in the lost wax process begins--carving the clay.

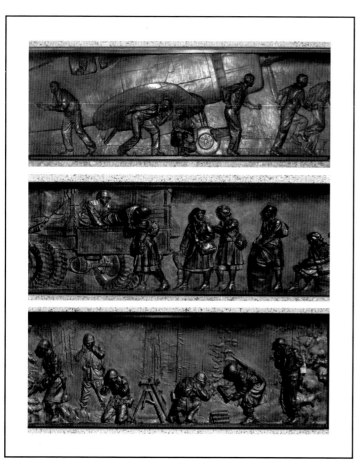

Insider's View

In October of 2013, the Federal government was shut down and the WWII Memorial was almost closed to veterans. The Memorial became a focal point for the media and the scene of some colorful political grandstanding by politicans and "anyone who had a point of view". WWII Veterans were allowed to visit the Memorial while it was supposedly "shut down" only due to some adroit negoitations. Honor Flights South Carolina and Oklahoma shown here with their Congressmen were the first Veterans to enter the Memorial that day. The WWII Memorial had become the focus of a political battle and protesters from every political stripe descended on the Mall.

Honor Flight™ is dedicated to flying Korean, Vietnam and WWII Veterans to see their memorials for free, The founders Earl Morse and Jeff Miller brought the organizaton from piper cubs to charter flights and there are now 142 "hubs" in 38 states across the country.

Senator Robert Dole, a World War II veteran, frequently greets the Veterans at the Memorial. They are also routinely greeted by a roster of distinguished visitors--Tom Hanks, Colin Powell, Senator John McCain, to name a few. Local volunteer groups wave flags, cheer and shake hands with the veterans. For this jaundiced photojournalist, visits to the the Mall have taken on a Normal Rockwell quality and I am a regular at the Memorial.

I spent two years photographing the construction of the WWII Memorial. The resulting book and work on the Mall has given me great pleasure, If you are visiting the Memorial, you will see groups of veterans visiting their Memorials due to the generosity of thousands upon thousands of volunteers.

The WWII Memorial is the most popular location on the National Mall, attracting almost five million visitors a year.

Honor Flight Chicago™ (above) flies one thousand veterans per year and conducts a ceremony each time. On the right page, the festivities include greetings, hugs music, dancng, family and reflection upon service.

OUR DEBT TO THE
HEROIC MEN AND VALIANT
WOMEN IN THE SERVICE
OF OUR COUNTRY CAN
NEVER BE REPAID. THEY
HAVE EARNED OUR
UNDYING GRATITUDE.
AMERICA WILL NEVER
FORGET THEIR SACRIFICES.

PRESIDENT HARRY S TRUMAN

The DC World War I Memorial

The DC World War I Memorial on the National Mall serves to commemorate the 26,000 citizens of the District of Columbia who served in World War I. The memorial was recently restored, and calls have been made to rename it the "National World War I Memorial." As with all matters concerning monuments, this minor proposed change is a major controversy. DC residents were outraged by the appropriation and so the plans have changed and Pershing Park near the White House will be the new site of the National WWI Memorial. The designs are already a cause of controversy.

Completely restored in 2012, it is a popular destination for families and small events You can see from the picture on the right that one of the reasons the Mall and its many fountains are hard to maintain is that the whole area was built on a river bed and is consequently always in danger of flooding.

Martin Luther King, Jr. Memorial

The Martin Luther King, Jr. Memorial sits on a direct axis between the Jefferson Memorial and the Lincoln Memorial, situating Dr. King in his rightful place among the country's great democratic leaders.

In his "I Have a Dream" speech, delivered on the stairs of the Lincoln Memorial, Dr. King promised, "With this faith we will be able to hew out of the mountain of despair a stone of hope." Following the trajectory of this quotation, visitors to the memorial pass through a mountain of despair and arrive at a stone of hope from which the figure of Dr. King emerges.

The entire project took over two decades, and the dedication was finally scheduled for the 48th anniversary of the "I Have a Dream" speech. Unfortunately, the opening ceremony was canceled and rescheduled as Hurricane Irene swept through the area.

Every new monument that graces the mall draws its fair share of controversy, and the Martin Luther King, Jr. Memorial was no exception. Complaints were raised over seemingly every detail of the memorial: Dr. King's stance was deemed "confrontational," the granite was the wrong shade of grey, and so on. Eventually, however, the importance of memorializing Dr. King as a champion of human rights and justice overpowered minor criticisms. On October 16, 2011 thousands of people came from every corner of the country for the memorial's dedication, a ceremony in which President Obama spoke of the tremendous impact of Dr. King's work.

Tidal Basin and Cherry Blossoms

The inauguration of President Barack Obama attracted over a million people to the National Mall, but there is an annual celebration that draws in a crowd to rival this historic attendance record: The National Cherry Blossom Festival. Tourists come from all over the world to the District each spring to view the trees in their short, two-week blooming period. In 1932, the mayor of Tokyo gave these 3000 trees to the United States as a marker of the growing diplomatic relationship between the U.S. and Japan.

The cherry blossom trees line the Tidal Basin, the man-made inlet that functions to regulate the water levels of the Washington Channel, storing the overflow from high tide.

The basin was dredged in the late 19th century, and today, the elegance of the Tidal Basin attracts many visitors. A sight sure to put a smile on every face is the hundreds of paddle boats meandering along the basin in the summer, gliding across the reflections of the Jefferson Memorial.

Thomas Jefferson Memorial

Author of the Declaration of Independence and third president of the United States, Thomas Jefferson was a man of great ideas. Fitting, then, is the monument erected in his memory, whose exterior recalls that of the Pantheon and whose interior boasts excerpts from Jefferson's letters and other sources, including the Declaration of Independence.

Designed by architect John Russell Pope and dedicated in 1943, the memorial drew criticism even during its construction. Today, however, the structure is widely celebrated as a cornerstone of the National Mall and attracts countless visitors, especially during the annual National Cherry Blossom Festival.

Rudolph Evans' bronze statue of Jefferson (right), added four years after the dedication, stands proudly in the center of the dome.

Franklin Delano Roosevelt Memorial

"Physical strength," spoke President Franklin Delano Roosevelt, "can never permanently withstand the impact of spiritual force." This statement certainly reflects a man's lifelong struggle with paralytic illness, a condition that he refused to accept to the end of his days. FDR almost never appeared in public in his wheelchair. Consequently, the memorial statues portraying him both in his chair and standing upright led to major controversy.

Dedicated in 1997, the memorial consists of four "rooms" that progress through the twelve years of FDR's presidency. Water plays a symbolic role throughout the monument.

Korean War Veterans Memorial

A plaque in front of the Korean War Veterans Memorial reads "Our nation honors her sons and daughters, who answered the call to defend a country they never knew and a people they never met."

On July 27, 1995, President Bill Clinton and South Korean President Kim Young Sam dedicated the Korean War Veterans Memorial, in honor of the 1.5 million Americans who served in the Korean War.

The structure consists of a circle intersected by a triangular wall. The wall is sandblasted with 2500 photographic images of troops from the land, sea and air during the Korean War. Nineteen stainless steel soldiers adorn the triangle, each one over seven feet tall. It is a moving tribute to our Korean War Veterans. The stainless steel sculptures are most interesting in snow and heavy fog.

The Korean War Veterans Memorial, Sculpture "The Column" by sculptor Frank Gaylord @1995.
Wall and Mural by Charles Nelson ©1995 and overall design by architect Cooper-Lecky Partnership.

Photograph: courtesy Carol Highsmith Collection, The Library of Congress

The Korean War Veterans Memorial was designed by Cooper Lecky Architects, the stainless steel soldiers in "The Column" by Frank Gaylord ©1995 and the "Mural Wall" was designed and built by Louis Nelson ©1995.

WOUNDED
S.A. 103,284   U.N. 1,06

CAPTURED
U.S.A. 7,140   U.N. 92,970

DEAD
USA 54,246   UN 628,833

MISSING
USA 8,177   UN 470,267

The Korean War Veterans Memorial ws designed by Cooper Lecky Architects, the stainless steel soldiers in "The Column" by Frank Gaylord ©1995 and the "Mural Wall" was designed and built by Louis Nelson ©1995.

Thirty Eight

The 164 foot long "Mural Wall" designed by Louis Nelson contains some 2400 photographs depicting the Korean War. There are nineteen stainless steel soldiers in battle gear created by Frank Gaylord. When the soldiers are reflected in the Mural Wall, they create the appearance of thirty eight. The number 38 is important as the war was fought along the 38th parallel and that separated North and South Korea. The trees that surround the "Pool of Remembrance" are also thirty eight in number

Plaques with the number of Wounded, Captured, Dead and Missing are embedded in the pool's border. The Korean War was one of the most difficult and hard fought conflicts in US History with 36,574 Americans dead and 103,284 wounded and 8200 missing in action or lost or buried at sea.

The Korean Community in the United States expresses its gratitude with wreaths and flowers and are perhaps the most ardent supporters of the Memorial.

The Korean War Veterans Memorial was designed by Cooper Lecky Architects, the stainless steel soldiers in "The Column" by Frank Gaylord ©1995 and the "Mural Wall" was designed and built by Louis Nelson ©1995.

Vietnam Veterans Memorial

Often referred to simply as "The Wall," the Vietnam Veterans Memorial honors the millions of men and women who served in the Vietnam War. The memorial consists of two walls totaling 493.5 feet; together, they list over 58,000 names of dead or missing members of the U.S. armed forces who contributed to the war effort. The memorial was designed to harmonize with its surroundings: The black, reflective surface of the walls gives the memorial a mirror-like quality, and the walls point toward the Washington Monument in one direction and the Lincoln Memorial in the other, grounding the names in history.

Creating a memorial for the most controversial war in U.S. history was, as usual, a contentious process. The memorial fund stipulated that the commemorative structure must focus not on the war but on those who lost their lives fighting it. Still, critics called Yale architecture student Maya Lin's design too nontraditional, and consequently sculptor Frederick Hart was appointed to create a complementary traditional bronze sculpture nearby. Hart's "Three Soldiers" features three members of the armed forces who appear exhausted from combat. The Vietnam Women's Memorial, designed by Glenna Goodacre, was erected to honor the women who served in the war, many of whom were nurses.

Today, visitors often leave commemorative gifts at the foot of the wall near the name of a friend or relative. The National Park Service collects and stores mementos left at the memorial.

An Insider's View

DEDICATION. In 1979, a group of Vietnam veterans founded the Vietnam Veterans Memorial Fund (VVMF), an organization that would work toward a national tribute for Americans who served the U.S. in the Vietnam War. On November 13, 1982, their goal became a reality, as that day marked the dedication of the Vietnam Veterans Memorial.

As 150,000 people flocked to the National Mall to participate in the dedication ceremony, members of the VVMF surely felt a surge of pride in the overwhelming support for their objective, despite the controversy surrounding Lin's design for the memorial during its construction. Thousands of veterans and supporters paraded down Constitution Avenue toward the Wall, some wearing old clothes worn in battle and others clad in bright, celebratory colors. Many members of the crowd had actually opposed the war, but that day all marched together to honor those who risked their lives to fight in it.

After ceremonial speeches and singing, veteran Jan C. Scruggs dedicated the memorial. The hundreds of thousands who had gathered on the Mall dashed to find the names of their lost loved ones on the Wall; hands reached out in every direction and continued to search well into the night. National Park Service volunteers and rangers help visitors to locate and make pencil etchings (page 96) of loved ones' names on the Wall.

MONTELEONE Jr · HARVEY D JOHNSON · JERRY LEE WALKER · LEROY WHITE Jr · JAMES G CONLEY · JAMES P DELANEY · HOWARD M STEINFELD · ERIC G HEROLD · ROBERT D PIERCE · CHARLES J RICHIE · DANIEL L CHAMBLEE · JOE E LOVE Jr · WILLIAM PHELPS · JAMES R THOMAS · JAMES E STEADMAN · JERALD W CARTER · RICHARD E GARRETSON · EDWARD J LOPEZ · ROBERT D MAYNARD · JAMES E PALMER · RONALD K SWEETLAND · JOHN E WINDFELDER · JOSEPH B ZIEL · MARVIN R KEETER · CHARLES P RUSSELL · RICHARD C PAWELKE · RANDY LEE CLIFTON · JERRY N DUFFEY · FLOYD D CALDWELL · WILLIAM BELL Jr · HERBERT R STONEKING · HENRY E EVANS · ROBERT E FURSTENWERTH · FREDERICK L HOLMES · FREDERICK J SUTTER · BEDFORD L DRINNON

LEE W BILLINGSLY · RAYMOND P DONNELLY · ROBERT R CECIL · MICHAEL A HILL
JAMES R LAYTON · EDWARD G HAYEN II · LARRY J YOUNG
RONNIE LEE GIPSON · GLENN E NOWAKOWSKI · JOHN A SPIRES · STEF
CHARLES F HAYNES · LESTER RUSHIN · LARRY E JAGARD · HAROLD McCASLIN Jr
THOMAS W REASOR · JOSEPH L RUZICKA Jr · FREDDIE L SLAUGHTER Jr · LUIS ALONZO · RO
DAVID N LARSON · CLYDE K NELSON · JAMES J SASSONE · WILLIAM G CHANDLER · PA
PATRICK A DECK Jr · HERBERT D STARK · EDWARD J BRUE · MARSHALL B COLLINS · JAMES W FU
MERRILL H MASIN · RAYMOND R REESE · DANIEL M RICHARDS · CHARLES P ROBERTS · W
BEN O SHEPPARD Jr · PHILIP H STEVENS · RAY E TANNEHILL · JERRY D VANCE
DAVID M THOMPSON · FRANCIS W TOWNSEND · JOSEPH E FRASHER · RONNIE HOLLY
LAWRENCE C DEAN · ORLAND J PENDER Jr · JOHN R OTZEN · GRADY T TRIPLETT · CATAL
ROGER E BEHNFELDT · RODERICK B LESTER · HARRY S MOSSMAN · WILLIAM J CROCK
THOMAS W STALEY Jr · MICHAEL W DOYLE · SAM G CORDOVA · GEORGE B WARING · RIC
CHARLES H PIPER Jr · ROBERT R GREENWOOD Jr · WILLIAM C WOOD Jr · FRANK G OLIVER II
DONALD J HANNING · DONALD F LINDLAND · RONALD F BOEING · DONALD A GERSTEL
STEPHEN O MUSSELMAN · ROBERT L HARLEY · JOHN L SMITH · MICHAEL P RICE
CARROLL T JACKSON · MELVIN E STEVENSON · KENNETH BUELL · VERNE G DONNELLY
MICHAEL S TUROSE · THOMAS O HORN · ROGER W CARROLL · DWIGHT W COOK
DANIEL V BORAM · PETER J VINCENT · ANDERSON · RICHARD B LINEBERRY
WILLIAM W COTTMAN · SCOTT E BIRKET · HERMAN GAITHER · JACK S BERGMAN
CHARLES W CLINARD · RONALD P DALEY · RAYMOND P DAVIS · TERRY W DEAL · WILL
TOMMY M HAWKER · ROBERT M KIKKERT · ROBERT T MOORE · EDWARD R McELENEY Jr
LANNY A YORK · RALPH L ROBINSON · WESLEY H ROSE · RICKY LEE RUCKER · JEFFREY L SCHELLE
WILLIAM J TERRY · RICHARD C TESSMAN · JOSEPH GRISAFI · ROBERT D ANDERSON
CARL O McCORMICK · PETER M CLEARY · LEONARDO C LEONOR · FRED MICK
WILLIAM M PRICE · JAMES L CRAIG Jr · JAMES D DUGGER Jr · ALLEN U GRAHAM
AUBREY E NOBLES · MICHAEL S PIXEL · CLAYTON W BLANKENSHIP · DANIEL P CHERRY
ROBERT W HAAKENSON Jr · KEVEN Z GOODNO · CARLOS A PEDROSA · MELVIN E WOL
DEXTER B FLORENCE · FRED OBERDING Jr · JAMES E SULLIVAN · JAMES D BROWN · RAYMO
ROGER R CHAMBLESS · DENNIS W FINNEGAN · RICHARD B FREEMAN · LOUIS O CALDERON
STEVEN D HOWARD · CHARLES A McSWINEY Jr · KENNETH J SPENCER · JAMES M STEVER
TIMOTHY A THOMAS · RONALD L VANLANDINGHAM · DAVID E WISCHEMANN · HOW
DELBERT R WOOD · WILLIAM L MILLER III · STEVEN E TAYLOR · JOSEPH F DENARDO · CL
ROBERT M BROWN · JOHN L CARROLL · ROBERT D MORRISSEY · FREDERICK W WRIGHT III
DOUGLAS T MANKA · DONALD G BREGER · CHARLES J CAFFARELLI · WILLIAM S HARGROVE
JOHN W RYON · RONALD D STAFFORD · CALVIN B TIBBETT · WALTER H TRISKO
JACK R HARVEY · BOBBY A JONES · RICHARD E BRUNDRETTE · ANTHONY C SHINE
LOUIS R TAYLOR · BILLIE JOE WILLIAMS · BILLIE JOE WILLIAMS · WALTER L FERGUSON
DONALD L REES · ROBERT THOMAS · RONALD J WARD · RICHARD W COOPER

GIANNELLI
NE MESSER
NAIMO Jr
PLUMMER
E ALDOUS
CARVALHO
LANIGAN II
RD GREEN Jr
G IMPSON
M M MILLER
HOWARD
WILLIS A TOOMES
DONNY RAY STEWAR
BENJAMIN F BA
ROBE
C GASSEN
JAMES R HOCKETT
WILLIE RA
CHARLIE L PARTIDA
SAMUE
THURMAN H
A CAHE

"The Three Soldiers" by Thomas Hart

Vietnam Women's Memorial by Glenna Goodacre

Lincoln Memorial

At 6'4'', Abraham Lincoln remains the tallest president to date. The stone statue of Lincoln, however, would tower over the original at an astounding 28 feet tall (if he stood up from that giant stone chair). Daniel Chester French's sculpture of the 16th president sits inside a Doric-style temple designed by architect Henry Bacon.

z

Built in 1922, the Lincoln Memorial honors a leader whose ideas inspired and reunited a struggling nation. The inside walls display inscriptions of Lincoln's most famous speeches, the Gettysburg Address and his second inaugural address. Martin Luther King, Jr. stood on the steps of the memorial to deliver his "I Have a Dream" speech in 1963, at the feet of the man whose presidency had led to the abolishment of slavery 100 years earlier.

West

Some vantage points require Presidential attention. For his inauguration President Reagan sent a letter requesting that the Architect of the Capitol grant Stephen R. Brown access to the Dome at dawn. The view was quite spectacular and certainly worth the effort.

East

As you wander the National Mall there is always a magnificent view in front of you. And a photographer who finds himself without a photograph need simply turn around and look behind him. As you can see, it just gets better.

Arlington Memorial Bridge

Dedicated in 1932, Memorial Bridge is both an aesthetic wonder and a symbol of unity. The bridge spans the Potomac River and connects two memorials tied to leaders of the Union and the Confederacy, the Lincoln Memorial and Arlington House, respectively.

As the story goes, President Warren G. Harding reinvigorated efforts to construct the bridge, which had been delayed since the original planning two decades before, when he found himself caught in three hours of traffic on the way to the Tomb of the Unknowns in Arlington, Virginia. The neoclassical structure initially functioned as a drawbridge, opening to allow barges to pass up the Potomac to Georgetown; this feature was abandoned, however, with the later upstream construction of the Theodore Roosevelt Bridge, which has no draw feature.

Designed by the prestigious architectural firm, McKim, Mead and White, the bridge spans 2,163 feet long, with nine arches over the river. Each arch features a bas-relief eagle, emphasizing the majesty of the bridge as a symbol of the reunited country. On the eastern end, two neoclassical equestrian statues flank the bridge. Its wide sidewalks make for a popular running and biking area.

Marine Corps War Memorial

While the Marine Corps War Memorial is dedicated to all Marines who have died in defense of the United States, the statue is commonly known as the Iwo Jima Memorial, as it depicts the famous moment from World War II. The successful takeover of the island eventually led to the end of the war in 1945. In fact, the memorial was inspired by Joe Rosenthal's Pulitzer Prize winning photograph, which depicted the inspirational raising of the American flag atop Mount Suribachi in Japan.

Designed by Horace Peaslee, the Marine Corps War Memorial was dedicated by President Eisenhower in 1954. The bronze figures stand thirty-two feet tall and occupy the same positions as the men in Rosenthal's photograph, raising a cloth American flag that flies twenty-four hours a day.

The granite base of the statue contains the engraving, "In honor and memory of the men of the United States Marine Corps who have given their lives to their country since November 10, 1775." On the opposite side is a quotation by Admiral Nimitz, who said of his men, "Uncommon valor was a common virtue."

Located at the entrance to Arlington National Cemetery, the memorial overlooks the Potomac River.

Part II:

Arlington Cemetery

Women in Military Service for America Memorial

Dedicated in 1997, the Women in Military Service for America Memorial stands at one entrance to Arlington National Cemetery. The memorial is the first of its kind, honoring all women who have served the United States since the American Revolution.

Structurally, the memorial mixes tradition and modernity. The outside of the building, designed by architects Marion Weiss and Michael Manfredi, subtly blends into the hillside with its stone plaza, tall arches and dark reflecting pool. Additionally, large glass tablets stand against the wall, understated but powerful in their engravings about the experiences of different servicewomen.

Inside, visitors encounter the magnificent skylighted museum area, which houses permanent collections and seasonal exhibitions that document the history of women in the military. The Memorial also hosts large photographic and art collections on a seasonal basis. The terrace level provides unparalled views up the hill to Lee Mansion and Memorial Drive looking to the Lincoln.

Arlington National Cemetery

Arlington House, which was Confederate General Robert E. Lee's mansion prior to the Civil War, sits high above the sea of tombstones that today is Arlington National Cemetery. During the Civil War, Union General Montgomery Meigs ordered that Union soldiers be buried in Lee's front yard, in part to prevent Lee, considered a traitor, from ever returning to the property again.

Today, the house serves as a memorial and sign of respect for General Lee, and those first twenty-six Union soldiers buried on the property mark the beginning of Arlington National Cemetery. The vast graveyard is the burial site of more than 300,000 military veterans and public figures, from the American Revolution to the present. Notable figures buried on the grounds include Pierre L'Enfant, Thurgood Marshall, the crew of the Challenger Space Shuttle, William Howard Taft, President John Kennedy and Senators Robert and Ted Kennedy.

One of the most visited areas of the cemetery is the Tomb of the Unknowns, which overlooks the District from a hill as a reminder of the importance of every individual who serves this nation.

The picture on the following page was taken from the roof of the Arlington Memorial Amphitheater on Memorial Day 1981. This photograph taken while Ronald Reagan speaking would never be allowed in today's security rich environment.

Insider's View

INTERMENT. A beacon of honor and patriotism, Arlington National Cemetery is an ever-expanding burial site for those who have served the United States. Due to limited space, however, the cemetery maintains the most restrictive criteria of all national burial grounds. Although the conditions for burial in Arlington National Cemetery are extensive and strict, the burial site still averages around twenty funerals per day.

Funeral proceedings at the cemetery involve a historic ritual for dealing with comrades fallen in battle. The casket is draped with the American flag, recalling the custom of covering the dead carried from the battlefield that began during the Napoleonic Wars. During the ceremony, riflemen fire three rifle volleys over the grave, echoing the sign used to halt fighting to remove the dead from the battlefield.

Perhaps the most famous funereal practice at Arlington Cemetery is the 21-Gun Salute, also known as the Presidential Salute. Cannon salutes, symbolizing trust and reverence, originated in the British Navy; a battleship would fire its cannons out to sea to empty its ammunition and signify its peaceful intent. Normally a bugler plays taps at the end of a ceremony.

The photographs to the left depict the funeral for Robert Tills, an ensign whose death marked the first casualty of the "War in the Philipines." His PBY was lost to the Japanese fleet flying to attack Pearl Harbor. While his loss was well-known and a destroyer named after him, his remains were only recently recovered in the hull of PBY #4. Tills was buried in 2009, almost seventy years after his death, with full military honors.

Pentagon Memorial

This permanent outdoor memorial, located southwest of the Pentagon, honors the 184 individuals who lost their lives at the Pentagon during the September 11 attacks. Opened on the seven-year anniversary of the attacks, the memorial was designed by Julie Beckman and Keith Kaseman. On September 11 of every year, the section of the Pentagon building hit by Flight 77 is illuminated with blue lights and an American flag is hung over the area. Additionally, memorial services for Pentagon employees are held on the anniversary date each year. The soaring stainless steel arcs of the Air Force Memorial are visible in the background from many vantage points at the Pentagon Memorial.

Air Force Memorial

The U.S. Air Force Memorial, located near the Pentagon and overlooking the city, honors Air Force personnel through three soaring, stainless steel spires. They evoke the contrails of the Air Force Thunderbirds, which can be seen above the memorial in the Missing Man Formation.

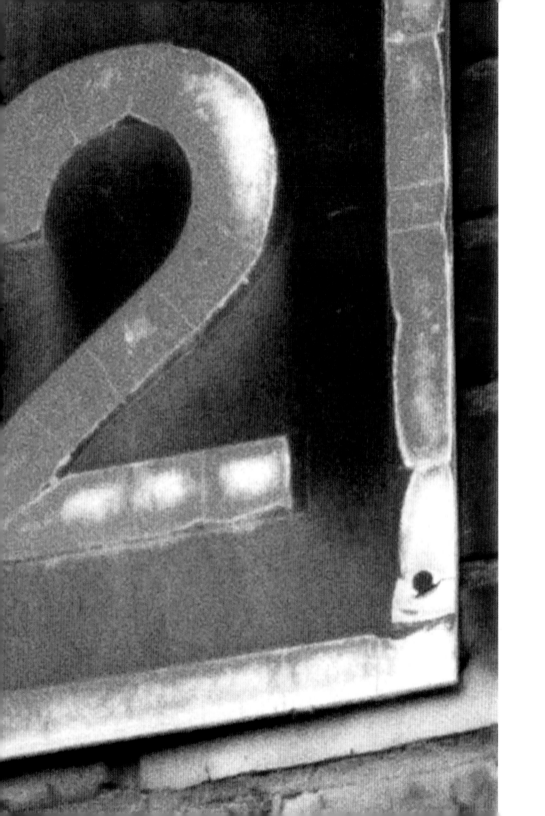

Part III:
The District

Dupont Circle

Central to the "old city" as planned by Pierre L'Enfant, Dupont Circle is one of the most vibrant and accessible neighborhoods in the District. It is one of DC's oldest and architecturally ornate areas. Many of the mansions built around Dupont Circle in the 1870s have been preserved, and there is still a trolley station (though no longer in use) underneath the circle.

Chess players, tourists, office workers, families and people of all walks of life relax and play in Dupont Circle Park, seemingly oblivious to the incredible traffic flowing by. Connecticut Avenue, one of the city's central arteries, runs directly underneath the circle through a tunnel constructed in 1949. On one side of the circle is Eastern Massachusetts Avenue, the site of a number of influential think tanks. Opposite that is Western Massachusetts Avenue, notable for Embassy Row, which extends up to the Naval Observatory and Vice-Presidential mansion.

Like that of many Washington neighborhoods, Dupont Circle's scenery and location are iconic. The 1998 film "Enemy of the State," for one, featured shots of the circle and traffic tunnel. Furthermore, Presidential motorcades frequently pass through, as the President often travels to fundraisers at the hotels further north on Connecticut.

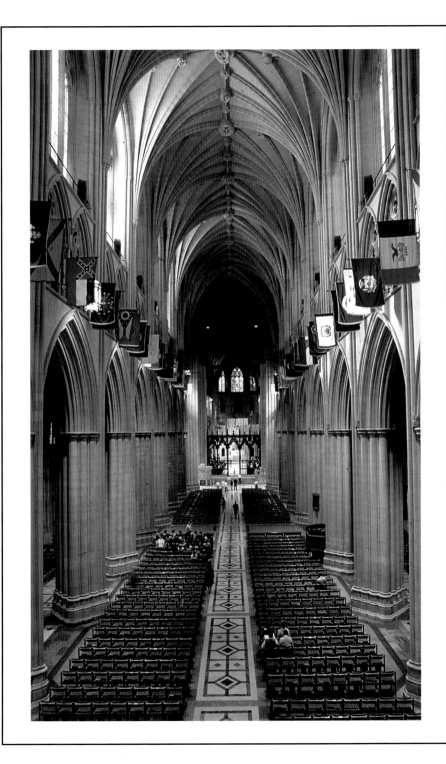

Washington National Cathedral

At first glance, visitors to Washington's neogothic cathedral might be surprised to find it was built in the 20th century. While the National Cathedral presents an exterior to rival the Notre Dame, it just recently celebrated its 100th birthday. In fact, construction was not complete until 1990 under the presidency of George Bush Sr. Like the Washington Monument, the Cathedral suffered extensive damage and is under repair.

Pierre L'Enfant's original design for the city designated an area for a house of worship for all people. The National Portrait Gallery, however, claimed the originally selected space, so the cathedral planning committee selected Mount Saint Alban as the new site. Visitors enjoy tours through the towers, as well as music by the Cathedral Choir of Men and Girls, which includes girls from the National Cathedral School and boys from St. Albans. Both prestigious schools are located on the cathedral close.

Georgetown

Nestled above the Potomac River, Georgetown is one of the District's most vibrant neighborhoods. As one descends Wisconsin Avenue, the elegant townhouses give way to the myriad trendy shops and restaurants of M Street. Georgetown boasts everything from chain stores and burger joints to upscale boutiques and restaurants and is, consequently, a favorite for shopping and dining. The Old Stone House is the oldest standing buildng in DC, erected in 1765. It is now a historic site run by the National Park Serivce.

Almost always busy and infallibly crowded to the point of bursting on Friday and Saturday nights, Georgetown features exciting nightlife. Just alongside the trendy bars and eateries, however, lie landmarks rooted in the rich history of this old tobacco port. Visitors to the neighborhood would be sorry to miss the historic house museums: Tudor Place, Dumbarton House and the Old Stone House. Equally impressive are the gardens at Dumbarton House, on the property called Dumbarton Oaks. Georgetown is home to celebrities, politicians and a prime location for movie sets.

Dumbarton Oaks

In 1944, representatives from the United States, the United Kingdom, the Soviet Union and the Republic of China met at this Georgetown mansion for the historic Dumbarton Oaks Conference. Less than two months of negotiations produced what would become the most important international body: the United Nations.

Today, visitors to the Federal-style house and estate spend hours strolling through the lavish gardens. The site is also a center for scholarship.

The adjoining neighborhood is known for its gorgeous houses and elaborate shrubbery.

C & O Canal

Where the Chesapeake and Ohio Canal cuts through Georgetown, mules still walk along the riverbank – today, however, the carriages they pull are full of tourists. Though the canal ceased to be active in 1924, many visitors enjoy rides down the historic waterway on canal boats. Park rangers in costume guide the tour boats, which can even be rented out for private use.

The canal spans 184.5 miles from Washington, DC, to Cumberland, MD. Because of the over 600-foot topographical incline between the two places, builders constructed seventy-four locks along the way, each of which would raise a canal boat about eight feet. In 1971 the canal became a National Historic Park, and today, the path alongside it is a popular trail for running, hiking and biking. Popular areas along the canal include Glen Echo Park, the Billy Goat Trail and Harper's Ferry.

Georgetown Waterfront

From early spring to late autumn, early morning to late at night, the Georgetown waterfront bustles with activity. Overlooking the Potomac, the waterfront is perfect for viewing high school and college crew regattas as well as the countless people engaged in boating and water sports. Thompson's Boat House attracts visitors looking to rent kayaks, small sailboats, sculls and bikes.

The harbor also features several popular waterfront restaurants, as famous for the view as for the food. Looking out at the Potomac River, diners see a series of historic bridges and buildings such as the Kennedy Center and the Watergate complex. In the summer, the elegant fountain in the middle of the restaurants at Washington Harbour draws adults and children alike to its steps, where musicians and street performers often showcase their talents. In the winter, the fountain is transformed into an ice skating rink.

Kennedy Center

"I am certain," said President John F. Kennedy, "that after the dust of centuries has passed over our cities, we too, we will be remembered not for our victories or defeats in battle or in politics, but for our contribution to the human spirit." How fitting, then, that this vibrant memorial for the revered president is a center for the arts: showcasing plays, musicals, operas, dance and ballet, as well as music of all genres.

Located across from the Watergate complex, the Kennedy Center occupies a beautiful strip of land on the DC waterfront. The terrace overlooks the Potomac River, and audience members often step outside during intermission to find themselves as equally impressed by the scenic outlook as by the extraordinary performances inside the building's walls. For rowers and boaters, the Kennedy Center stands as an impressive landmark from the Potomac.

Opened in 1971, the Kennedy Center was designed by architect Edward Durrell Stone. Despite the extremely high cost, which grew from $10 million to $60 million during construction, critics from media and national organizations alike supported the building. As a national memorial, the Kennedy Center receives federal funding, but its cultural and educational initiatives are paid for almost entirely by gifts and ticket sales.

Chinatown and Penn Quarter

From Caps games and concerts at the Verizon Center to the plays at Shakespeare Theater, to exhibits at the Smithsonian's American Art Museum and Portrait Gallery, a host of cultural options make the Chinatown and Penn Quarter area of Washington a vibrant area of the city. Additionally, the neighborhoods are rich with restaurants, bars and smaller theaters, and a number of farmers markets and cultural festivals take place there throughout the year.

Nationals Park

The first major "green" stadium in the United States, Nationals Park is a LEED-Certified structure. Nationals Park provides panoramic views of DC landmarks that rival the attractions of the stadium itself, as the Capitol and the Washington Monument are both visible from certain areas of its 41,888 seats. A recent addition to the DC waterfront, the stadium officially opened on March 30, 2008, when the Washington Nationals took on the Atlanta Braves. In Major League Baseball tradition, President Bush threw the first pitch, a ceremonial act that preceded a victorious opening game.

Southeast Development

Well into the 2000s, Southeast DC had little in the way of shopping, dining and cultural attractions. In fact, city residents recognized the area largely for its elevated crime rate and resulting tragic media reports, even in the section just below the U.S. Capitol. In 2005, however, construction of the new baseball stadium for the Washington Nationals began, and with it came sweeping changes to the Southeast waterfront neighborhood.

When the ballpark opened three years later, the surrounding area was virtually unrecognizable. The July 2007 demolition of parts of South Capitol Street had brought the area closer to sea level, and a newly painted, six-lane road had emerged. Developers had seized and replaced the nearby housing projects, shabby shops and rundown storage areas with new commercial structures.

Completion of the stadium, though, by no means marked the end of development in Southeast. The city council and developers predict that the introduction of new office space, housing units and retail stores will continue well into the decade. In 2009 the city built a water taxi pier at Diamond Teague Park, and the Ballpark Boat has been bringing people across the Anacostia River to the southeast corner of the ballpark ever since. Another water taxi service, the American River Taxi, has been operating to the ballpark from the Georgetown waterfront since 2011. Plans are still in the works to build another taxi pier at The Yards, located several blocks east of the stadium. These services are the first steps in a water taxi system connecting various points along the river, including Georgetown, National Harbor and Alexandria.

National Museum of the US Navy

The Navy Yard is an active military base and you will need to have an ID ready to visit but it is one of the best kept secrets in Washington. As one of 14 Navy museums throughout the country, it is the only one that presents an overview of U.S. naval history. Permanent and temporary exhibitions commemorate the Navy's wartime heroes and battles as well as its peacetime contributions in exploration, diplomacy, navigation and humanitarian service.

Udvar-Hazy Center

A bit out of town but worth a mention, this adjunct to the downtown Air and Space Museum displays thousands of aviation and space artifacts, including a Lockheed SR-71 Blackbird, a Concorde and the space shuttle Discovery. It also has an IMAX theatre where wide screen shows are on the hour and is convenient to Dulles Airport.

On the Move

Named after John Foster Dulles, the Secretary of State under President Eisenhower, Washington Dulles International Airport (top and far left) may not be the closest airport to the District but is, perhaps, the most architecturally renowned. For shorter flights, residents choose the closer Ronald Reagan Washington National Airport (middle left), located just across the bridge in Arlington, Virginia.

Union Station (left), the historic train station and shopping center, occupies a prominent site on Massachusetts Avenue, near the Capitol.

Kilroy

And who was Kilroy? Rumors have it that he was an inspector in a Philadelphia ship building firm or that he worked in China as a maintenance engineer. This easily drawn cartoon became a symbol of quality control and American presence during World War II. There are many Kilroys who have claimed to be the "Real Kilroy" and there are several websites devoted to his legend. The designers of the World War II Memorial chose the Kilroy cartoon to symbolize the quality and care they put into building the memorial. You can find the cartoon at the entrance to the maintenance stairways at the World War II Memorial. Quite a few people have reported him to the Park Police as "graffiti." Welcome to Washington!